Finding Love's Way

*A poetic exploration into the
deeper rhythms of love*

ALSO BY SARAH KATREEN HOGGATT

When the Questions Come
When the Ink Runs Dry
In the Wild Places
In His Eyes
Learning to Fly
Encountering the Holy

Learn more at SarahKatreenHoggatt.com

Finding Love's Way

*A poetic exploration into the
deeper rhythms of love*

Sarah Katreen Hoggatt

Spirit Water Publications
Salem, Oregon

Spirit Water Publications
P.O. Box 7522
Salem, OR 97303

Library of Congress Control Number: 2015914124

ISBN: 978-0-9729460-5-6

Cover and interior design by Sarah Katreen Hoggatt
Author photograph by Erin Zysett

Also available as a hardback and Ebook

Manufactured in the United States of America

For those beloved
who walk with my soul
and for those who give me
the great privilege
of walking with theirs.

Contents

III

IV

V

VI

Acknowledgments

When writing about love, I have found it best to have your main support be some of the people you think of first when you hear the word "love"—people who exude the quality in their very presence, in their words, and especially in their actions. It has been an awe-inspiring experience to have such wise and kind souls with me on this journey and I have learned a great deal from their examples. Not only have they been there to edit and comment on every piece of this book, they have cheered me on, given me sacred space beside them, and shown me love throughout. I am *deeply* grateful to them all. If every writer had such beautiful souls in their lives helping them along the way, there would be far more books about the deeper rhythms of love.

Thank you to my editors and friends *Bob and Sue Henry* for all the times you told me how much my words meant to you and for all the times you read a line or a whole poem and told me I could do better. The effort you've put into these pages has been a precious gift and I am so grateful you said yes. In return, Bob, you now hold your wish in hand. As this is my largest book to date, may you enjoy many years of new material to share with those lucky enough to hear you speak. And Sue, let's take a walk in the garden again.

Thank you to my editor and friend *Gil George* for your critical eye, your honesty, and for further drawing out the essence of my words. I am immensely grateful for your prodigious skills as a writer and poet and for sharing them with me so faithfully in the midst of a tumultuous year. This Thanksgiving, *you* get to cook and *I'll* edit.

Thank you to *Tricia Boyle* for walking with me through every stage of this journey—from writing the poetry to holding the finished volume in hand and everything in between. You have been the candlelight around the labyrinth of this book. Thank you for your continual care and support, for your inspiration, ideas, and opinions. Your presence in my life has been a most treasured gift and through your companionship, these pages have been shaped into what they are today. Next time, you get to go first.

Thank you to *Carole Spencer* for the common sacred space and companionship I sorely needed as I worked on putting this manuscript in order. I am deeply grateful for your hospitality and the sharing of your home, yet even more so, for always sharing your heart. Thanks goes to you also for inviting me to walk the labyrinth that day in Indiana—it was the inspiration for the entire undergirding theme of how being love is very much like the twists and turns, the journey inward then outward, of this most ancient symbol of growth and prayer. It's a gift to have you nearby once more.

Thank you to *Zarrah Buitron, Annie Glen, Jessica Murdoch,* and *John Erik Pattison* for reading through the finished manuscript and giving me your thoughtful feedback. I greatly appreciate the time and effort you put into it and am eager to return the favor someday.

Thank you to *Erin Zysett* for using your graphic design skills on the labyrinth image, for helping me fine-tune the page design, and for once again assisting me in creating a cover to be proud of. I believe that is two drinks I owe you now.

Thank you to those *friends and teachers of love* who inspired me and gave me something to write about. Your love for me and my love for you is the most beautiful thing I know. I wrote about it in every line.

Most people listed here including myself have had close family members and friends be seriously ill, stay in hospitals, or die while we've worked on publishing this book. We have each learned not only to value every breath we take and to let go of the trivial, but, most importantly, that our greatest gifts in life are the gifts of those we love and to actively treasure those people today and every day after. It is my dearest wish that through these words, others will learn this central lesson while they still have opportunity to live it out on their own journeys of life alongside those they love and the God who loves us all.

Introduction

I became aware of how similar the experience of walking a labyrinth is to learning the deeper rhythms of love in a soft-lit room in Indiana with a labyrinth laid out upon the floor. In my mind was the core of this manuscript which I'd brought with me to put in order in the sacred space of some time away. As the path beckoned me on into contemplation and prayer, I stepped forward while talking with God about love. By the time I found my way to the center of the circle and back out again, I knew I had been given a gift of understanding upon which this whole book would be based.

The ancient symbol of the labyrinth has been around for over 4,000 years and is a powerful tool used to pray and connect with God. Although a labyrinth can take many different shapes, it consists of one circuitous path winding around in an intricate design, in and out of a circle, eventually arriving at the center then winding back out again. It's a way to pray with our bodies, to be in the here and now giving space to our thoughts while communing with God, to walk out our questions and perhaps hear some answers. In a labyrinth we go inward and outward, coming around to different lessons at different times, feeling far away, then coming close, all the while learning to not judge where we are. Through our steps, we relearn lessons in new ways, take the time for deep breathing, deep listening, and to hear what God is teaching us. The labyrinth I have chosen to use for this book is the same one I walked in Indiana: a smaller version of the one built into the floor of Chartres Cathedral in France, constructed in the early 13th century and rich in spiritual symbolism.

As I took the turns around the labyrinth asking God my questions, I was moved by how the truth of love was working itself out through the movement of my feet; the experience of both the labyrinth and love are so similar. As in the path of the labyrinth, sometimes love feels intimately close and at others, we feel so far away from where we long to be. Though love seems like a confusing maze, it is in truth the one winding path we all walk in our daily breath, teaching us one step at a time through all the twists and turns, guiding our growth as we find love in the center of our divinity. Learning love is a journey of being who we *already are*—walking the path we are already on, and expressing love in the outer world. We are embraced by the experience of love no matter where we are.

Relationships are the most important things in the world. The love I share with those around me is the greatest truth I know and the one I have the hardest time expressing. Even the word "love" seems trite and shallow in comparison to what it represents and what I feel. Love includes warm affection, though it goes far deeper. Love is the coursing divine energy connecting us all, the light shining in every soul and in every created thing. It's the beautiful light we feel with God and the light I see shining in the eyes of those I cherish. Part of my own journey has been learning to see that same beautiful light in myself, to understand that love is an ever-flowing fountain running abundantly, more than I'll ever need and more than I can ever give away. I must first value this gift, though, value who I am, and be centered in myself before I can share love with others and be embraced by their love in return. We can only give what we have first found within ourselves.

In truth, there are no words for what I feel coursing inside my soul. Sometimes I feel love so strongly my heart aches with the fullness of it—as if I'm trying to contain a powerful force of energy a hundred times my size and I'm unable to do so. True love, in its deepest sense, sees no labels and has no fear. Love knows neither shame nor needs certainty, but is openly expressive and alive. It's an incredible gift to live out of, and through it God has taught me to see with deeper eyes to a wider view and a world far beyond—one our souls know but our limited minds are slow to grasp. In this wider world, love points to the truth that God, ourselves, and love are all like one flowing tide, truly inseparable one from another. God created and is the beauty inside each one of us; the gift of love is that shared recognition of the same yet unique light we each possess. When I say, "I love you," I'm not only expressing the deep and abiding affection I feel for you, but also rejoicing in the profound connection we share. After all, love *should* be expressed; we all need to know we are loved. Hopefully my love is not just in my words, but also in my actions and in how I treat those around me—the places where love is always shown best. I want you to see it in the way I look at you and for you to sense it when we're together—to sense how the beautiful expression of the divine in me utterly loves the expression of the divine in you.

As "love" is my favorite topic, and one which fascinates me to no end, I wish there were more books to read about the deeper truth of love but there are not. (A notable exception is *The Mastery of Love* by Don Miguel Ruiz.) Nearly all books about love are about the romantic variety. I find this extremely frustrating for as beautiful as romantic love can be, the path I want to read about and search for myself is the deeper rhythms of love underlying all the labels. I want to search out the gifts of affection in deep friendships, between God and the soul, and the love I feel inside going far past whatever names I can give it—the love for which we are created and for which we long. Thus, this book is *entirely* about that deeper kind of love so other readers coming along may have a wider selection from which to choose. Although I know many of you will identify with some of the poems in a romantic way and I fully support you in that, none of them were written with romance in mind. Deep affection and longing to share love with ourselves, with each other, and with God is a universal experience and comes from the same heart. One of the incredible things about poetry is the words can take on a whole new meaning for the reader than the author ever intended. I invite you to see yourself, God, and those you love in whatever ways speak to your own soul.

The poems in this book have been placed into storyline order and have truths to convey both individually and as they move from one to another. However, the poems may also be read in whatever way seems best to you: page-by-page or at random, the choice is yours. I know the right words will find you at the right time.

While I walked the labyrinth in Indiana, God gave me a phrase I have thought about ever since: "something to be and something to give." What I thought was learning *about* love turned into learning to *be* the love I already *am*. Now, even as I continue the journey, I have something to *give*. The words within this book come from the deep places inside me where I still ask the questions, consider the thoughts, and learn to see and express the great love within me. It is my hope that by walking alongside me, these words will express what is inside you as well. Though the labyrinth is ultimately a solitary walk for each person, through these pages we can walk the labyrinth of love together. Join me in taking the first steps.

With love,
Sarah Katreen Hoggatt

I

In Every Word

In every word
spelled out

but itself not
needing to be said
in any declaration.

It's always felt,
always known,
always shared between us
in sacred space

if we have the eyes to see
and ears to hear

for we could not meet
as we do
on any foundation

but love.

The Jewish and Pakistani Divide

My neighbor
from Pakistan
creates such aromas
in her kitchen
which I love walking past
breathing them in.

Then one night,
she knocks on my door
with a plate
of delectables
in her hand
I have never tried
and my knees
must find the floor.

We speak few common words
yet I look inside myself
to find a way
to be as loving as she.

Devotion

Beautiful problem,
I give myself to you

in abandon

following the road
in neglect of all else

giving to this one thing

which I think may take
its first breath

and live.

Underneath

Unlovable...
perhaps
second rate or
simply not
worth keeping.

The hidden fear
held beneath
people
come near
but not close,
will love
but not hold.

My heart cries
aloud
for hands
for love—

the tears fall
down
my cheeks
yet I turn

for I did not
mean to show
the pain
the fear
the longing

of love
on my face.

God Came Along

What are you doing here?
　　I'm sitting.
Alone?
　　Yes, alone.
Why didn't you invite someone along?
　　I didn't think they'd come.
You didn't want to hear "no" again.
　　No, I didn't.
So why are you talking to me?
　　Because I knew you'd say yes.

God Knows Best

God's hand
held firmly over my mouth
ignoring my muffled excuses,
my wanderings of self-doubt,

wrapping my fingers around a pen,
he pushes paper before me

urging me
in not so many words

to shut up and write.

Your Face Haunts Me

Your face haunts me—
perhaps a phantom
of what I wish could be
and I keep this longing
   inside my heart

unless you can hear
my eyes shouting
aloud—
   seeking you out
   in silence

   not understanding
   what is

   or why my soul
   wants you beside me

but knowing
your spirit speaks
   in the quiet dark

and still I must go on

without you.

If You Were a River

If you were a river,
what would you look like?
A river, God?
Yes, a river.
What do you look like?

I'm turbulent—
the water is hurling up white,
churning and kicking and racing
hitting the shore
lifting logs and branches—
I feel stormy, a little angry,
and I've overflowed my banks.

Hmm...
What do you see underneath?
Under the water?
Yes, at the bottom of the river.
What do you see?

The flow of water is
powerful and strong—
yet it's calm.
Oh! There's a seed!
There's a little seed on the riverbed!

Take it and hold onto it.
What will it become?
Wait and find out.
The seed is for you.

Right Time

Like a good book
on the shelf
waiting to be read,
to be opened

only when the student
is ready to learn the
wisdom it holds,

so will you
come
when you are ready,

finally finding the
courage
to rise
and run

in the wide
open field.

Source of Words

I hold love close
though it burns my hands
and casts into shadows
the places where it has carved away
with its sharp knife
hollow canyons
longing to be filled

and if it's into this emptiness,
this living pain of love,
you pour in strength
where I cry my tears,
a power of words
where I go to grieve,
then it's the pain, the loss
inside me
welcoming these phrases,
to give voice to the grief,
to open up the empty places
where I hang the tears

so others might feel
the sacredness of their sorrow,
their struggles,
their own flow of love.

This ache of hurt
opening the well of
life-giving water—

I will be grateful
for my heart being torn

urging me on

to invite all those
who are thirsty
to come and
drink this love,
this source of power,
strength of my pain.

Thus I will cry the tears
going beyond myself
so others' fields may be
watered with the words
I am driven to release.

Transmitting

Walking through the woods one day
    in mountains green and deep,
kneeling down to hold the cord
    our souls delight to keep.

In honoring our connection,
    I felt your spirit strong,
and I reached down into myself,
    a power pure as song.

To your heart I sent this gift,
    the strongest one I know—
pulsing light of love within,
    around you—a peaceful glow.

Embracing you with all my heart
    to cast this powerful spell,
to calm your spirit, give you joy,
    your worries stilled and quelled.

I do not know if you felt my love
    as you went about your day,
but it was there just the same
    and it is there to stay.

Out of the Dark

Lying in the dark,
drum pounding
muffled in my ears—
you come and kneel
beside me.

I look up
into your face
as you take my hand,
uncurl my fingers
and reveal
a young shoot of
unfolding leaves
fresh and green,
vibrantly growing
in my palm,
shining
in its own light

and as I gaze
in wonderment
at this beautiful
creation,
you find my eyes
and express,

You're a life-giver.

That is who you are.
You grow life
and vibrancy
in the world around you.

And as the drum
quietly rolls on,
we look again at
the plant still growing
in my hand
with outstretched fingers

finding where
my soul
is joining your
divinity.

Beyond the Creed

It's not the
Nicene Creed
binding us
together,
nor a common theology
or religious practice,

but it's our existence
as souls
one to another
as we gaze
into each other's eyes
bonded together
by our divine image.

Holding our spirits
in mutual wonder
and delight in God,

we take a step
across the line
and embrace,

for religion must
always step aside
and give way
to love.

Low Tide

Finding our way to the sea
across the bridge
and through the shifting sand
flowing between our toes,

we soak in the wanting space,

valuing the unseen grace
as shells turning in the
light of the sky,
shimmering in their glittering light
and their journeys of being

as we wash
in the give and take
of the turning tide.

Holding the Words

You said my name
out of the depths of feeling—

and though your arms
were around me

I still do not understand
what you meant

and the words haunt me.

The Forbidden Dance

There's a man dancing
body leaping
out the beating rhythm
as if around a fire
wild in the trees
released and free
embodied exuberance
flowing—

I watch, fascinated,
envious
of the life within him,
a forbidden fruit
brushed on my lips

and I am left wondering
with eager eyes
and hungry arms
if it feels as good
as it tastes on my tongue.

If You're Upset

If you're upset,
lower your expectations.

Can I dare to love like that?
Is it really daring at all
or simply letting go
of what's holding me back,
a laying down of the lie
that real love could ever
come with conditions

and instead live
with an open heart,
accepting the gift
of what comes
and letting love pour out

like the open petals
of a flower
soaking in the rain,
flowing fragrance
indiscriminately
to the breeze?

Clicking Circles

What are you up to God?
I'm just wondering
because the circles
seem to be clicking
and the stars aligning
in ways I have only
seen in visions
of this fantastic person
I could be,
an image only
in my fondest hopes
into which I dared not step.

Yet now the door
beckons open
and one stone after another
is laid before my feet.

And so I must go,
must step through
into a wild world
drawn from created vision

into a very real
life I may just
dare
to live.

II

Presence

Caressing the sunset
with my eyes,
breathing in the
fresh scent of the
first rain while
watching the drips
dropping from the leaves,
hearing my favorite sound
in all the world.

Holding pencil in hand
shaping the contours
of a four petaled flower
and standing heart-bare
before the rolling thunder
as it rumbles through me,
humbled by its power
uncontrolled.

When I stop and pay attention—
when I quiet my inner world
and wake up to
the one around me,
soaking in its nourishing soul,

I pray.

What Do You Look Like?

God, what do you look like?

What do you think?

I don't know.
I've had many images of you
    before
but they always change
and I let them go.
And though I hold onto a few,
I carry them with open hands
knowing they can never even begin
to encapsulate who you are.

So I think of you
and see unfathomable mystery,
a dark light I can't understand
and I wonder,
what do you look like?

What do you hear?

You. I'm pretty sure I hear you.

Keep listening.

Willing to Be

My soul understands
things which words despair to share
knowing they can never
communicate across the page
in any comprehensible manner
what I need to express

yet the words push at my fingers
willing themselves to be
under my hand
for they know
I am terrible at telepathy
and they have to get out.

Bubble

Standing
amidst the
coursing tidal
wave of terror,
the crushing
anguish
of untold suffering
taking place in
this world,
pain—so much pain—
as if *I* had suffered—

I raise a shaking
hand to
create
a hedge
around my soul,
to push it away,
lest the horrendous
truth
tear my heart
apart
as I cry
aloud in the dark
a self-cast spell—
whispering in tears

bubble...

bubble...

bubble...

When Rocks are Falling

God,
it feels like
the rocks
are being thrown
from multiple directions
one after another
again and again—
breaking, bruising.

I fall to my knees
and cry out
for mercy,
for the rocks to stop,

for relief
where only your
tender hands
touch me
and only your voice
can reach me.

That's where I pray to go,
where I long to find you
when the last

    rock

       falls.

To Love

Whatever it means to love,
I'm sure it's not this—
blind revenge, anger before compassion.

"Has no one condemned you?"
    We are so quick to condemn.

"No, no one Master."

I look up, embarrassed,
with surprise in my eyes
to find no judgment in his gaze
as dust still hangs in the air
where the stones fell and the feet fled
of those who could not lie to stay.

"Neither do I condemn you.
Go on your way and be restored."

Looking again to be sure
of what he said,
I find freedom in his tears
and I know what it is to love.

Him

Dust billowing out
around my feet,

I watch as Jesus
kneels down to
touch the leprous skin.

The man, stunned,
gazes up and I stare.

He touches!
He touches...

Then he reaches
out and touches me.

Garden of Grace

I lived for myself,
no need for effort
beyond my own world
but now there is you
standing at my gate
with expectation

and I have to turn
and look around
seeing with new eyes
the weed patch
and the overgrown roses
climbing the walk.
I hear your questions
and run my fingers
across the dust
on the stone bench.

What kind of place
is this to invite
someone else into?
Have I scoured
deep enough,
dug my fingers into
the earth far enough?
Walking in the grass,

I drag out the weed barrel,
push up my sleeves and
pick up the rake
and the shovel,
lifting a thank you
to God for giving me
a reason to look
with new eyes
and for the pleasure of
inviting someone else
into my garden of grace.

One Sun

What does my love matter?
What does one person's expression
of love, one soul's
flow of connection count?

Yet the power overflows me

and I *am* love
and love loves

open and whole heartedly
with wings like the rising sun
and the heat of the desert noon

shining forth
in this one
wild
and expressive life.

Throbbing Oneness

I lift up the
blanket of shallow reality
to lay my hand
upon the pulse
of throbbing Oneness,

the vibrant connection
running up through my body
to you, to all,

and all that I can only see
when I close my eyes
and lay back in its arms

to dream the dream
of what is always here,
all around
and within.

Anyway

You have
what the world
needs

but
does not
want.

You have to
give it
anyway.

To Show You Magic

I want to show you magic—
the northern lights shimmering
on the near horizon,
the sound of the trees talking,
the flowers dancing,
the energy in every living thing
moving, changing,
and to know that everything is *alive*.

If I can do this,
if I can open your awareness
to a sparkle of the light
you can see beyond the seeable,
hear the song beyond the hearable,
the music grabbing
hold of your soul
and taking flight,
learning to soar along,
your heart lifted,
your spirit singing,
hands moving to
play the turning light,

if you can see this
and dance along,
even once in a while,
then I will have been able
to pass on the most priceless gift,
the one my own soul longs to know:
the gift of seeing God.

Watching God

I see you there
clapping your hands,
swaying in rhythm,
delight etched on your face,

and as I turn to watch
where you gaze,

I realize we are not
merely your creations,
the beings you wanted to build,

oh no,

we are your *art*.

Then You'll Know

If we do not have eyes to see,
how can we love a painting
or admire the sun?

If we cannot sense in our skin,
how are we to gently brush
a petal across our face
or squeeze the sand
between our toes?

If we cannot smell,
how are we to know
the deep pine scent of the woods
or the roses blooming in summer?

Just the same,
if we do not see ourselves as loveable,
how can we see God
as a being who loves?
If we refuse to know
our true souls,
kicking our spirits around
like refuse in her realm,
how can we understand
what we truly are?

If we blind ourselves
and refuse to see
and value what God knows,
the beauty with which
our beings inside are lit,
what is God to say but,

I see you
and I know who you are.
I'm waiting for you
to see yourself
and then you'll know,
you'll truly know,
what I see,
why I sing,

and the ocean of love
you live in
every day.

Dear Self

I love how you're willing to say
what needs to be said
yet in a few short words
you can make a whole room
burst out laughing.
You search for wisdom,
hungry for a depth of understanding,
bravely walking a road of your own
ever firm in who you are
and what you're here to do,
yet already knowing enough
to be the holy fool—playful, mischievous,
freely taking adventure by the tail
while challenging yourself to be more *you*.

You are courageous in your "no"
and so I love how your hands,
eager to lighten a load
and your feet to ease another's way,
also search with curiosity
and follow through with faithfulness,
feeling others' joys and sorrows
in your tender heart, ever supported by
the immensity of strength within you.

You, my dear one, are lit with an inner light,
sparkling with an abiding love,
an aromatic rose,
a star in the sky we call God.

Be Still and Know

High up in the oak tree
leaning against God,
my feet hanging in the air—

a branch wraps around me
holding me closely to itself
and to the arms of
God as I rest here
in peace, shalom,

wanting no more
than to watch the leaves wave
in the breeze,
sense the sun on my face,
and to feel God's heartbeat
in every breath I take.

A Writer's Greatest Risk

I gaze in your face
and I confess it's easier to see
in the face of one I love

but the beauty of your soul
is exquisite to behold
and I look at it
with my deeper eyes
and find it marvelous.

You are one of the greatest
gifts of my life

but you just don't go around
saying that to people

so the words go unsaid
as I falter at the door
of this intimacy of truth
wishing I could take the risk
and say the words
instead of just write them,

praying one day I'll find the courage
while regretting not having done so still.

Divine Wings

I reach out to you
in the solitude of my heart
and whisper your name
across the space divide.

You're like a bird
freely flying
choosing to alight
where you will
when you will

and though you flee
when held too tight,

when you land
on outstretched fingers,

I catch my breath
and hold you close
for I know not
when I'll see you again.

Why You?

Why you?
Why your face?
Your eyes?

We live
in two
different
worlds

bonded with love

yet look
two different
ways.

Why
can't I
just let
you go?

III

Look Again

Stretching out my hands
hoping they might take mine in return

but their backs are turned
and they do not see.

Oh, *why* did I agree
to pay such a price?
Salty tears proclaim
it was much too high!

Look again
and you'll see
my heart break,
opening up
to hold the universal ache,
encompassing the pain

as it turns into the water
for the sacrifice
I hardly want to give
anymore.

Tentacles of God

If I could make you
turn towards me,
to invite me into
your sacred space
to walk with you,
speak with you,
share the load,
I would do it.

But you don't turn.
You don't raise
your head to see
where I grieve.

I have so much
to give you—
my hands
are extended
cupping your face
as you sleep,
held in deep longing
and yet…

you still turn
your face away.

Why?

Learning

God, what they said,
what they did,
how they acted—
it was so hurtful and
I'm left picking thick thorns
out from where
they stuck them in,
one after another,
and I want to explode!

You have to remember, dear one—
don't take it personally.
Their choices are not about you.
They're fighting battles
you know naught of.

I'm trying not to take it
to heart God,
but it's hard when I feel ignored
or when their mean words
are falling down my face
like the tears I later cry.

I am here holding you.
I know, yet it still hurts.
I know.

We All

We all have needs
more than flowing water
and succulent food for our mouths

but don't ask me
to admit mine
for I know you will not
choose to meet them

and I will be left starving

just as I am now
but with the additional
twist of the knife
that you know.

Realizations

Beware of your judgment
for you will be bound in black
by the labels you cast.

Beware of your dread
for you will be imprisoned
behind the bars of fear
you sink into the ground.

Your anger will be the food,
the poison you ingest into yourself.
The revenge you plan and inflict,
the hate on another soul,
another piece of yourself,
will be your desired guilty verdict
you declare on *you*.

Be wary of the chains you hold
for they will wrap around your feet
and drag you down
into the violence within yourself.

You shred your own soul
when you refuse to see
someone else as a person,

a soul dearly loved by God
and you want to throw them away.
You throw yourself away.

Thunder Roar

Thunder rolls
flattening me to the ground
and making my
eyes go wide.

Humbly bowing
and soundly
put in my place
under God's mighty hand,

the flash of light
and reverberating roar

teach me how
infinitesimally small I am
in God's universe

and how much I need
to know it.

Tree Language

Leaning my head into
the bark of the trees,
my face cushioned in the moss
and my arms wrapped
around the trunk of my brother,

I listen to the tree
speaking to me
of deep and ancient things,
of things words cannot say

and they listen to my heart
pouring into their sap
what I dare not say aloud.

They hear me.

Not Enough

God, help me
when digging my fingers
into the earth
is not enough,

when knowing
we are connected
through the soil
on which we all walk
or lie beneath
fails to satisfy.

Forgive me when
I stand on the shore
of my soul
and long for the water
beyond the dam,
a vision of nurturance
beyond my sight,

when *I* am the earth
and *I* am the water
and you—

you are the light
shining in
and illuminating
us all.

Somebody Saw, Somebody Knew

Somebody saw,
somebody knew
the golden roads
through the wood
where my feet trod
in the early dawn.

Somebody heard,
somebody smiled
at the heron's flight
along the river's shore
where my canoe
gently flowed in the rising current.

Somebody touched,
somebody loved
the smooth rocks
in the creek
where my legs waded,
caressed in the glorious sunlight.

Somebody saw,
somebody knew
the blowing grass
in the field
where I danced
among the wildflowers.

Bonded Together

There's a cord between us
    hidden underground
    and no matter how the years may pass,
    we stay together bound.

We may seem to walk our ways
    and let each other go,
    but the bond won't break or joy forsake
    as round again we grow.

Though many times in daily life
    it is hard to see
    and I forget that you are there
    quietly loving me.

But when I hear your heart-filled voice,
    I feel the cord anew,
    a warmth, a fire, a joy to my soul,
    this connection I share with you.

Stepping Out

That deep connection
to not be unafraid

but to love
with all that you are,

to lay your hand on another soul
and to accept the pain
as well as the delight,
to make the sacrifice
as well as be lost in the joy.

One very well might be
worth the other,

we'll just have to
remain open and find out.

The Sun and the Rain

Two seeming
opposites
trying to
overtake
the blue,

yet I see
a rainbow
with the sun
and the rain

like the yes
and the no—

never an either or
but together
a flowing river
finding its path,
moving its course,

changing the way

I swim in the currents
and gaze at the colors
turning in the sky.

You Remembered

You remembered
the color of my coffee—
the amount of cream
I like to sip
on a cold morning.

You remembered
my favorite cuisine—
a dish of Thai
over a fire
with a cup
of delectable
peanut sauce on the side.

I'm amazed
you remembered,
that you cared
enough to know.
I never knew
how nice it could be
to have someone
who remembers.

Simple Gifts

A fire to warm,
a blanket to feel,
a book to read,
and a friend nearby.

It's the simple gifts
I find to be
the most meaningful
and the most profound.

Before Me

You sit before me
gently there
without suggestion

and I know
what I must do

for sometimes we
need to see
the truth of our lives
in the eyes
of another

before we truly
see it for ourselves.

Mosaics

Piles of colored tiles
scattered before me—
the remains
of a picture
once created with
love and care

yet now jumbled
in a careless heap
before my feet.

Dropping to my knees,
I hold the tiles
in my hands,
tears falling
for what once was
and filled with grief
for what
I was compelled
to destroy.

Is there a new picture
amidst the shards of clay?
Does it end here

or do I take a risk,

pick up
the shattered pieces
and form
a new mosaic
of life recreated?

Gift of Stone

Is this a gift, Lord?
Something to help me
with the gift
you first gave?

Did you create
    this stone
    this wire
    this cord

to wrap this soul
in an aura
    of love
    of clarity
    a cloak of protection
to strengthen
to heal
to give peace

room to breathe
to just feel *me?*

Was it your hands
tying it around?

Is this stone a way
    you formed
    in the earth
I had too limited
an image of you
to see?

The Soul Walks

The feet hurry,
the soul walks
to sit down
in the company
of a friend.

The feet hurry,
the soul walks
the trail of the
labyrinth,
pausing, quiet.

The feet hurry,
the soul walks
to listen to God,
to talk, to *be*.

The feet hurry,
the soul walks.

Breathe In

Breathe in the sharp scent,
breathe in the little flowers
filling the crevices of your lungs.

Breathe in the aromatic cadence
of the ocean's flow
and remember how
the smell of the breeze

flowing over the sand

changes to burnt wood
right before the rain tips down.

The Fire

Alone and shivering,
I go sit
and hold up my hands
by the fire
out on a desert night
surrounded by
the empty expanse
of a sea of sand—

a light for my soul
to sit beside,
to feel the heat
upon my face.

Staring into
the depths,
the flame of love
where my soul
finds its peace
embraced in solace,
I lie on the ground
for rest and comfort
in the circle of heat
under a chilly night
as the stars gaze down.

You then come
sit beside me
holding the silence,
the thoughts unspoken
but not unsaid.

Looking over at my face,
you hold out
your cupped hands
opened to reveal
flaming light
as I gaze intrigued

and you speak
impassioned words,

You come to seek
the fire to warm
your longing soul
yet you do not
understand
the deepest truth
that the fire is not
something to seek.

You blaze before my very eyes
for you yourself
are the fire.

Your soul the very flame of love.

IV

How Do You Live as Love?

How do you live as love, God?
How do you breathe in,
breathe out, along with
the rhythm of your heart?

How do you walk this road
while holding the pain,
the sorrow,
as well as the joy?

How do you let go
when love is all that you are?

My own heart wants to drown
in the overwhelming power

of this force in me
you call Love.

All the Love You Need

Dear One…

Yes, God?

Take a look inside yourself.
Are you letting love itself be who you are
or are you letting what you love
define what you see?
You already have all the love you need.
It's an overflowing fountain
inside yourself
connected to the energy of all.
You don't need their love
to give you a reason,
love just is.

What about when love hurts?

Ah, yes.
Love can be the hard pain,
the need to be steady,
the call to remain open
when the connection is unseen
but it's also the respecting of self
as much as it is honoring another.
Love can sometimes be the "no"
as much as it ever is the "yes."

You have a choice in how you are treated
for you, too, are worth the loving.

Sometimes, all times, you have to let
someone learn the lessons
they choose for themselves
even while loving them.
The growth of their journey
as you take your own
is equally valuable
even when you don't understand the why.

Take pleasure in the simple act of loving
no matter what is returned.
You'll learn to see me there
for there is nothing that is not me
and you'll find yourself
looking into my eyes,
coming into tune
with the pulse of breath
that is love.

Withered Leaves

Raising withered leaves
to the sky,
my stalk bent over,
parched for water,
for life, for the uttered
nurturance of time,

my fallen petals tell me
with stark reality
it's time to reroot myself,
to move on,

that a plant untended needs
to find a place
where life is received,
nurturance given and effort made,

not just a place
where life is given away.

Language of the Hands

I will
believe
your words

when

your hands
speak
the same language.

Vulnerability

Raising my head
to meet your eyes,
chin trembling—
determined
not to cry
despite the tears
I can feel
running down my face—

you look back,
no judgment…
just compassionate observation
tenderly handing
me comfort
as you lay your hand
in the open wound,

pain I've tried to hide

but shared with you
as I sit exposed,
shaking in trust,
overwhelmed
in the loss
of what is missing

and the gift
of choosing
to be open
about it
with you.

Garbage Catches the Light

The old and abandoned
where the garbage
catches the light

and you go down
a dead-end street
of overgrown yards
and tiny houses
because you might as well
and have nowhere else to go

only to find a bridge
over a flowing creek of life
with trees arched over the rocks
and a duck splashing along

knowing God is there
when you did not.

Lying Here

I lay my head down
by the river
watching the water
flowing—

the sunlight drifting
across my body
as the curls of the grass
wave over my weary limbs
as, half-heard,
the birds sing
a soft song
in the trees above.

The air, the life,
fingering my skin,
bringing back to life
all that fell asleep
and floated away
on the current

now returning in the eddies
reminding me why I lie here
and what I'm waiting for.

Sacred Space

My heart floats
in on a melody
and I can sense God
sitting in a chair nearby.

On a cold fall night,
I can feel her here
in quiet companionship
sipping a glass of wine
and running her hand
along the back of the cat.

And I,
I lay here
feeling myself renewed
in the gift
of such common
sacred space.

The Real Question

Am I really
listening to you
and learning
about who you are

or am I creating
a character God
moving you around
like a puppet on a stage
with words I can foresee,
unchallenged
and self-serving,
painting the scenery
to suit my desires

instead of seeing you
in all your majesty
to the point
where I kneel,
trembling, down,
splayed out on the ground
with tears of repentance
in my eyes
for thinking I could define you

and you have to tell me
to fear not,
to get up and lift my face
so I might dare
to look upon you
perhaps once again,
perhaps for the very first time.

Awakening Breath

Once the crocus has
broken open,

once the shell
comes apart
releasing life
into the world,

such a thing
can never be
pulled back within
itself or reigned back
into an ancient darkness.

It must awaken
sending its breath forth
to animate the living.

Taking Love's Risks

Love—
the more I experience,
the less I understand it
and the more it means to me.

There must be love without fear
but it stands on shaky ground
calling out into the wind
looking for a home
and I hesitate whether
to welcome it in.

But let me hold you closer
than I've ever dared
and I'll try to learn
to not be afraid of it.

Your Presence

Your soul
tugs at my sleeve

flitting in and out
of my peripheral vision

turning my head
to catch a glimpse
of your spirit

always walking
in the shadows

never letting me
forget your face,
your eyes before me,

and though we seldom touch
the skin of our hands,

I'm unable to forget
the bond of love
once created
and held forever.

The Gift of Being Seen

Sitting on the sidewalk
playing my guitar,
strumming a tune
with eyes half-closed,

your feet pause before me,
to listen, to inquire?
Swaying in rhythm,
hearing the single beat of the
dropped coin in my cap,

I look up—
meet the ebony pools
of your eyes—

and see you
love
the music.

Wood Fire

Smell of the wood fire,
sipping soup
at a table,
just being...

Savoring cups of tea
with you

as the heavens fall
onto the leaves

beyond our world
through the window pane.

Here You Are

I have watched you for months—
your bare branches
blowing against the wind
before a backdrop of steel grey sky
and now here you are—

all verdant green, bursting with life,
your new leaves stretched out
to embrace and to know
with hope for whatever might come.

And here am I,
standing at the altar of your birth
slipping a dress of the same
verdant green over my head,
my arms stretched out,
raised to the sky,
hoping for a new life,
a new rebirth of my very own.

Sink Down

Sinking down my roots,
my fingers winding their way
through the dark soil of the earth,
the loamy richness
taken in my veins,
breathing in the cool dark
ever deeper, ever longer,
finding my course while
drinking in the rich nutrients,
searching for the ungraspable God,

knowing it's especially
in the dry times
when I must seek
out what feeds me,

my roots expand
into the groundedness of self
and the unmapped depths of God
to where the wind
cannot blow me down.

Sink down roots,
sink down.

Bag of Seeds

Why die with a bag of seeds
hanging
at my side?

I dig away
the earth with my hands,
the dirt tumbling
across my skin
leaving behind the hope
what I have to give
will one day grow
beyond itself

and when God
takes back
the white canvas

some morning,
it will only be
to turn it upside down,
verifying
I've already poured it out,
intent on
leaving behind
everything
he first poured into me.

Love Flows On

So many people
telling, pushing
on me what I
should be doing
for them in the guise
of a benefit to me,
tugging at my arms,
pulling at my legs,
wishing I'd take their ropes,

not understanding
I walk unfettered
for God, for me,
and if I give
it is freely, in love

as the waterfall
cascades down
nurturing the ferns
in its spray,
flowing down
past the rocks,
the barriers,
the log jams
seemingly in its way.

I flow on in my purpose
unperturbed
by your demands,
around, over, and under,
on and on,

listening only
for the call of the sea.

In You

Sitting by your shores,
I gaze inside
and see your strength,
your tenacity like a rock
holding its place
in a fast moving stream,
yet yielding and kind
as you wash your waters
around parched feet
cooling the throat
of a tired traveler.

Not needing to
prove your worth,
you simply flow along
watering the plants
along your banks,
nurturing the fish
swimming in your waves
yet you change the course
of land and hills.

You live in a power
not like the thunder
but as the rain
changing the landscape
over which you roll
seeking new paths,
new streams
of questions
in which to flow
and experiences
of bringing the soil
along on your journey.

The Calm in the Midst of the Storm

I lay back in your arms
in a sea of ocean calm.

Resting as you hold me here,
trusting in your wisdom,
in the voice inside myself,

unafraid I'll stray too far away
in my journey of questions
for you walk with my wandering soul
and I can lean on you
when the questions
are too weighty for me to hold

and so I float here in your arms
where you are watching over me,
lifting me in your hands of prayer.

Here, I can just *be*—
with the ocean lapping at my sides
for you are the water surrounding us
and I am free to fly in the storm.

When Love is No Longer Patient

Is there love without limits
when I don't like the rules?
Is there love without condition
when it goes back down underground?

Do I wait it out in the storm,
in the cold and alone,
still believing that love
is the bond connecting us all

or do I cut my losses
and find my way
knowing full well

I can do nothing
but love?

Beneath the Surface

There's so much in life
we do not see
beneath the surface—
only visible
if we let ourselves
sink down,

down where questions rule the day
and answers can only be felt,
not said,
nor even fully understood.

Yet when you come back
and sit on the ash
of what you thought you knew
with the sun's warmth on your back,
the memory stays with you
and alters what you see.

River Prayer

Sitting beside the river
tin cup in hand,
dipping into the flow,
the water cold and clean
crossing my lips
and into my veins—
pressing my face into
the current,
feeling it wash against
my face, my hair
flooding down around me.
The sun warms my back
as water runs down my neck
dripping over my body.

I raise my hands
in gratitude,
water streaming down my skin,
my face turned toward the sun

breathing in—breathing out

my one prayer
in this place that you, too,
are somewhere along
the riverbank
in the fragrance of the flowers,
the shade of the trees,
with a tin cup of your
own in hand
overflowing with life-giving water
and your face, dripping,
turned to the sky.

God in My Dreams

Walking in a hilly valley
filled with cream colored rocks and sand,
gravel swirls like rivers
stopping and starting in turn—
no ground truly solid.

Swirling underneath my feet,
the whole land flowing down like water
and I, lost, stranded in the middle,
I can't get out!

Scared of the gravel pulling me
down underneath the current,
I cannot breathe!

To the left
at the edge of the valley,
I see a dappled grey horse
trying to get through all the rocks.

Again, the ground churns beneath me!
I try pulling myself up
onto a nearby outcropping of rock,
gripping the sides with my fingers,

when I turn—

the horse is there
standing next to where I cling.
Climbing onto its bare back,
I find a tentative handhold,
lie down and circle my arms

around its neck,
my head laid down against its side.

As the horse moves through the rocks,
the heat from its body radiates
into my skin and its muscles
contract and stretch beneath me.

Absolutely safe, complete trust
pours over me—
the only thing in this place
to depend on,
not carrying me *to* safety,
but *being* safety
and I, at rest,
occupying the space I am meant for,
fall into peace.

Sabbath

Pattering down
on outstretched leaves,
I wake to the falling rain
brought in by the morning air.

A quiet day, a restful day,
filled with empty sacred space
to tune a deaf ear
to the clatter of nothings

and instead turn to the one Voice,
only the one Voice
as if untying the only bridge
to my holy hallowed island
where I plant a tree
and watch it grow,
to embrace the unthing
that is everything
and to find the blurred line
where it's no longer clear
where I end
and God begins.

V

Let Them Grow

Sometimes
you need to leave
to find yourself.

Sometimes
you need to shake
out the roots
to let them grow.

Sometimes
you have to let love
fly out of your hand
for it can only live
in an open palm.

The Circuitous Road

With a backward glance
to all the paths
my feet have walked—

what seemed to be
mismatched and fragmented,

I now perceive to be
but one circuitous road
winding round,
the twists and turns
guiding me to where
I knew not
I needed to go.

If I can dare
to let the journey give me
what it knows I need,

not trying to contort it
to my own expectations

but letting the perceived difficulties
be transformed without labels
until they are
what they were meant to be

and the joys
equally free to be
the teachers,
the Divine fingers
pulling me open
to contain the experiences
of life's pilgrimage,

I may be able to let the gifts
flow through me
without judgment,
leaving behind
what was never mine to take
and taking in
the immensity of beauty
all along the road.

God in the Gutter

I've seen God
in the beautiful:
giraffes walking the
African savanna,
a purple iris heart,
mighty mountains
and grand cathedrals.

But what about God
in the ignored?
The tree struggling to grow,
the cracked sidewalk?
Is there light?
New life in the old,
the cut down?
Is there God
in the common,
the broken?
Is there beauty in what is abandoned?

I believe God *is*
in these things
yet I'm driven to look and why?
I need to know she's the bridge
at our dead ends,
that he's the flowing river of life
under all things,
the light reflecting through
what we throw away.

I need to know
because *I* am the forgotten corner,
the common dandelion,
the creek running below.
I am the weeds in the gap,
the trash on the ground,
and the left behind words.

I need to know the mosaic
of beauty made of such things
so I can hope there is a mosaic in me.

Maybe what I'm asking is not,
"Is God there in the unlovely?"
but, "Is there God in me?"

Love's Shadow

God, it seems the more I learn
about love, the less I'm holding on to.

What has changed for you?

Love is now less of an idea
and more of an experience,
not so much a gain
but a release.
Love is a feeling the way
waves represent the ocean,
swirling and frothing
out of the great deep
and I find myself choosing to
walk through the surf
letting my head sink down
below the light,
lost in a Being I don't understand
rather than stand at the shore
thinking that's all love is.

Yet I see people just wandering
there on the sand in fear
and it breaks my heart
to watch them dying for something
they already *are*.

But how can I express this
when what I feel surrounding me
is beyond words, beyond easy conveyance,
a core of radiant divinity
pulsing, glowing, and bright
like the light of the sun
blinding our eyes,

a living energy I feel shining inside
but can't fully see
and all I can do is *be* the love we are
for even these words cannot convey
the heartbeat of love's aliveness
flowing in us all.

And what do you think would
convey this truth to them?

Not a what, a who.
You find your way
to teach this to us all
and I trust you do
even when it seems like you don't.

All I wish to ask is you let me
be a part of it.
Let me be a bit of you in the world.
Let them feel your love in my shadow.
I would consider it the greatest
honor ever bestowed upon me
if they saw a ray of your light
in my face.

Oh, my dear one,
you don't see it,
but you already are
a beautiful bit of me
in this beloved and light-filled world.

What Matters

It's not the belief
that matters
but the love—
the compassion,
the heart of giving
when no one else is looking.
It's the light
in a person's eyes,
the truth in the heart,
not the theology of the mind.

In the silence,
I take a breath,
look deep in your eyes,
into the depths of your eternal being
and in that sacred space,
the common ground of oneness,

I see the beauty,
I see the great light,
and I gaze in awe
at a loss for words to express
how the Divine in me
utterly loves the Divine in you.

Remorse

The song came on
and you asked me
if I would sing

and I said no,
ever since wishing
I would have said yes

and let you hear
the sound of my voice
unguarded in expression
and open to all
that could have been.

Sending It Out

Overwhelmed by
feelings I cannot say aloud,

I pull out a sheet of paper,
laying it out line by line
for God and I to see—

an expression of the inexpressible,
love hidden from view
when it has nowhere else to go.

I send it out through written sound,
working it out in the words.

If I Could

If I could reach out
and touch you,
I'd stretch out my fingers
knowing now what a gift you are.

If I could speak words
and know you hear me,
I'd beg your forgiveness
for thinking for one second
love was not here.

If I could be in your company
and see the look in your eyes
telling me you know the depth of soul,
I would wrap my arms around you
and hold you tightly to myself
as if to never let you go.

The Depths of Prayer

Your fingers running
along my back,
my head laying
on your arm

looking into your eyes
as I confess
those thoughts only heard
by your heart

and you say my name
and caress my face
as tears well up
and flow from my eyes

while you wrap your arms
tighter around
to remind me

how beautiful we are
and how much I need to share it.

It Wasn't Only

It wasn't only
for the leper
Jesus touched.

It wasn't only
for the woman
Jesus spoke.

It wasn't only
for Jerusalem
Jesus wept.

Why are we
so fearful
Jesus would never
    touch,
    speak,
    and weep
with us?

Why are we
so surprised
when he does?

When We Rise

With a steaming cup of coffee in hand,
I stand before the open kitchen window,
a cool morning breeze washing
over my face

as I listen to the birds greet the sun—
the drip of the sink
and the calling of the train
adding their own chorus
to a truth far deeper

we are made new
every morning

and every night die a little death
to be reawakened to life
the following day when we rise.

The Artist

The pencil hanging
in the air
over the paper—
considering
what eager eyes
would like to see.

A chrysanthemum?
Perhaps an ocean scene
or a fish in the water?

Yet I am drawn
to create
a simple cabin
in the woods
where I can see
a beautiful lake below
as the sun rises.

Torn between
fulfilling their need
or my own,
I hear,

"Don't be the artist
people expect you to be.
Be the artist
that you *are.*"

And so I smile,
draw my pencil
across the paper
and begin.

Until I Tried

Staring at the face
shaded in pencil
looking back at me,
amazed at what came out
under my hand,
the result of time spent
in creative bliss
moving graphite around a page.

Yet, too many times
the pencils remain in the drawer,
the boat is tied to the dock,
overwhelming affection—held in,
and the opportunities given, left behind,
never taken.

How much beauty has been lost
because I sat when I should have stood,
held my tongue when I should have spoken,
and put away when I should have created?
How much brighter would the world be
if my love worked its way out
through my hands and my mouth
instead of only held in my heart?

The drawn face stares back at me
in artistic testimony,
reminding me how I didn't know
I could draw
until I tried

and willing me to take out
the pencils of my heart
    so I may dare
    to draw life
and love
as well.

Tantalizing Questions

The knowledge creeps inside
like a delightedly unexpected guest
inviting me to take
a new turn in the path,
to gaze at a new horizon

filled with tantalizing questions
like a ripe mango on my tongue,
the tangy, sweet flavor
intoxicating my mouth,
inducing my steps
as I explore new directions
under the sun

of the immensity of God within
and all around,

of what I'm here to do,

and the gift of who we are
to each other.

Without Limits

I wish I could capture
this feeling forever,
found in the flow of life
tumbling across the rocks
into the emerald pool
where I am held,
melting into the One
coursing through all,

feeling myself pulled
beyond my vision
into a greater truth
we are *all*
nourished and held
as we stand and love
without limits
as the water flows on

and if we take it in,
letting it become part of who we are,
part of every breath we take,
the steady beat of our inner hearts,
we will be one with the current
even when the water is cold
and we are gasping for breath,

the sun will pull us out
making us forget
why we ever wanted to leave

and birth in us
the longing to return.

Acknowledging the Real

I reach out
and take your hand

holding it before our eyes
acknowledging the real
between us

hoping to communicate
what I don't dare to say
and what you will not say:

that there is love here—
nourishing, life-giving love

and I just hope
it feeds you
as much as it does me.

The Other Way

It's harder to let myself
be loved
than to do the loving

but the joy
in watching someone
dance with delight
at my presence
or reading words telling me
I am their treasure
awakens in me
an aliveness of connection
my soul knows I need
as I laugh to know it
and cry happy tears.

Do I really take it in,
letting their affection
soak through me
like a plant taking in water,
giving my heart permission

to be held

as I lay my sick head in their lap,
their fingers stroking my hair
in a priceless moment
of compassion and care
to be lived out in vulnerability.

We can go through life always loving,
always giving, but will never fully live
until we open our hearts the other way
and let ourselves be loved.

What is Truth?

Truth is a touch,
truth is a voice.

Not a description
of sinews in the hand
or the connective tissues
of the fingers
but brushing my face—
it's the feel, the breath
in my chest.

Truth is the echo of your voice
in my living body,
the love flowing through me,
the very energy
vibrantly alive.

Clouds of God

Swaths of white
stretched out above
as if painted on a background
untouchably beyond.

Below, a ball of cloud
I could brush with my fingers
rolls across the sky
and curls around itself,
shifting in space

as if inviting me
    to interact,
    to experience

the reality

that God is not
painted high above

but is rolling through us,
wrapping around our fingers,
shifting our view of the world
and our perception

of the shining light
kissing the earth.

Letting Go

You
who were
once
known,

you
who once
saw light
shining—

would now look
eyebrows raised

to the top of the bridge
where I stand
stepping over the rails
spreading my arms
and falling

through certainty

into the mysterious depths

of the churning
water

far below.

No Labels for This

As I've lost one
bit of ground I stood on
and am not comfortable
fully losing myself to another,

I hold out empty hands
with a loss of identity.

Gone.

My fingers grasp around
in the dark
for something I *can* hold,
a spark of something to light the way
but a voice in my ear
speaks to me what my heart
has already known—

"No rock will save you."

No rock to hold,
no identity to keep for myself,
no labeled theology
to guide me by,

only a blind trust to
rely upon,

a fire of twisting energy
burning inside,

and a Divine voice
speaking in my questions.

Brother River

Brother River—
the same water
flowing in you
overtaking your banks
flows through my spirit
making us one.

I brush my hand
across your currents
and you caress
my feet
in your majesty…

an exchange of embrace,
of love, respect,
of undying devotion
as we tread each other's souls
touching and holding,

hearing the whispered words
as we flood ourselves
into being.

Release

Having turned the corner
and released
what is no longer in sight,

the burden put down at last,

I take in a deep breath
of fresh clean air,
liberated
from the labels
that no longer matter
and the expectations
that were never of help.

Instead, I see
as though tracing a stream
through the desert valleys
that it's our vulnerability
in "brokenness"
when we show
our profound beauty

and in our release of "perfection"
we discover
we are whole.

Changing Light of Night

With a quiet spirit
I hold a candle in the woods
casting a light on the leaves overhead

and though I know I stand in what
I can't fully voice,

my soul calls out

and somehow I know
yours heard me,
that we are more
than brain and heart,
we are eternal spirit
deeply connected
with far more to our beings
than we can see

and it is out of this place
of quiet inner knowledge
within the wind and calls of night
I find my peace inside
and the strength
to love and speak
the Divine gift

as I lift my inner eyes
and raise my candle to the moon
grateful for what
we always were
and always will be.

The Open Gift

What a gift
    to find another
    who moves to the rhythms
    and asks the questions
    thriving in our searching journeys.

What a gift
    to share the conversation
    and feel understood
    being just who we are
    amidst the limitless wonders
    of a God we cannot name.

What a gift
    of releasing love
    we are able to give
    when we let go of our fear
    and show our true forms
    in all their beauty,

    falling in love with each other's souls,
    opening to the gift
    we've known before
    and discover once again.

Under the Knowledge of the Soul

Each soul sees a part of me,
knows a light in my soul
coming alive beside them
and when they're gone,
that part of me dies
like a field of flowers with no stars,
no moon to show their beauty

and I see how
we are connected
with one another far more deeply,
more intimately,
than we have yet guessed

to where there's no division between us
and when I think of that,
I find my way
seeking the embrace of God,
my soul bare in her arms
as I cry hot tears into her shoulder
for reasons I can't explain

but to say the knowledge
of how deeply we are in each other's souls,
how much of myself there is to lose,
and the you that's inside me
is more powerful than I can contain

and so my human heart
cries under the knowledge of the soul
as I'm wrapped in the One
who understands this truth
and knows why I must cry
far, far better than I.

Living

To walk in the dark
without seeing
but trusting,

to guess at understanding
without facts
but knowing,

to move into the light
without walking
but going,

and to shine in this truth
without holding
but being.

To see beyond
human form
into the greater expansion—

we all know this way
deep in our souls.

I Love You

These words I have not
dared to say,
this feeling I've swallowed
and held inside,
pushed down
so I could be safe

now bursts forward
at last,
unsuppressed,
and so I say it
aloud—

"I love you."

and take the
consequences.

VI

The Sound of the Rain

I love you.
I love you in
the sound of the rain
flooding down in the
early morning,
the cool breeze
rubbing up against
my face,
water cleansing
my soul anew
pouring out
as my body falls
open,

raised hands
to embrace your spirit
washing the world
in nurturing life,
and I rejoice
in this renewal
of plants, of breath,
of the illuminated soil
soaking in your being.

Sending down my roots,
your palms against my neck,
I raise my hands like leaves
to the heavens,
washed in your presence,
feeling you flow inside.

Oh, how I love you.

The Face of God

If you want
to see
the face of God,

turn

look at the face
of the person
standing
next to you.

God
will be there
turned toward you,
looking at herself.

Learning to Express

I just had to tell you
    I love you.
I had to say it out loud

for sometimes

you *do* go around
telling people they're one of the
greatest gifts of your life
because they *are*
and what do you have to gain
by holding it in—
never telling them

your heart is dancing
when you see them
and at the end of the day
when you thank God for the
joys in your life,
they are there in your mind,

thoughts of them
inspiring in you the only words
you can muster before such
glorious light—
    the thank yous,
    thank yous,
    thank yous

rolling around on your tongue
and falling out before the God

who shows herself
   so richly,
   so beautifully,
in the lines on their hands
and the skin on their face.

So let me tell you once more:

   I love you,
   I love you,

   I
     love
        you.

The Priceless Moment

Souls proclaiming their truth,
sharing the powerful force

embraced—

love, free to be the energy
encircling through and around ourselves,
strengthening the bond
already beyond breakability
or even understanding,

lighting the world
like a thousand stars
inside my soul.

This is the priceless moment—
the one for which
I'd scour the heavens
just to have back
around my shoulders
in the here
and now.

Soul, Speak to Me

Soul, speak to me of love.
    We search for what is without
    believing we have something to gain
    when we have nothing to gain
    and nothing to lose.
    How can we find what is already here?
    Love is flowing out of us,
    an eternal source
    that must be found within one's self
    before being given.
    To love another is simply seeing
    ourselves more clearly
    for in truth, there is no division
    between you and I.
    Love is merely the divine breath
    shared between souls.

Soul, speak to me of yourself.
    Do not qualify or try to measure
    that for which there is no end.
    You are an eternal being,
    there is no end to your soul.
    Remember, in your growth
    we are all constantly unfolding
    into more of what we already are,
    ever new and forever ancient.
    Let go of the need to identify
    for what is within you
    cannot be labeled.
    A power beyond words,
    you carry the universe inside your soul.

Sometimes Love is Silent

Sometimes love
is silent,
hidden and veiled
behind the trees
in the forest,
unwilling to walk
with you
in the open fields

and as much
as the absence
of love brings ache,
a deep loss
of what came so close,

you must take
the step forward
    beyond the safety of the woods,
    beyond the shadow of the trees,

complete in yourself

knowing what
exists in love
    is never lost,
    never wasted,

but you have to go on

and leave the gift where you found it

for it cannot travel with you
and was never meant to stay.

Ropes for Two

Among the trees
I walk the path
without you

for I would rather
walk together

than drag you along
on a journey
you never truly
wanted to take.

Even if you thought you did,
even if you opened up and told me
you wanted to enjoy the view
together,

I see the truth in your choice
    of the ropes,
      not my side.

So I release the bonds
from out of my hands,
letting you take
the needed responsibility
for yourself and your time

as I make a new choice
    and take new steps

birthed from the newfound
truth of my soul.

Understanding

God,
please help me
understand
this life

and give me
peace
when I don't
understand…

which is
most
of the time.

Turning

People step out of your life
and you don't want
to see them go

but you have to
turn your hands—

releasing them back
into the river
from whence they came.

They are not yours to keep

but to watch in gratitude

as you would
gazing up

at the stars

turning in the sky.

Death Knows

Death knells surround
and I am strangely comforted.
Everything is settled, finished,
the door has been closed
for every person below my feet
and I wonder on this day
when death at last
has become a friend,
what *I* will do
when I finally invite her in.

When my last tear has been shed
and echoes of my laughter fade away,
I want to be able to look back
and see at least a small portion
of the leaves my tears have nourished
and the blossoms my laughter has lifted.

But even if this small request is not to be,
if I am to die blind
to what my life has meant,
I will still have loved,
still have sung my soul to the heavens,
will still have lain in the river of God.

This must be enough for death
for even if I do not know,
death will know when
the offering is complete.
Death knows when
the value of a life
is worth the giving.

Soaking in Solitude

Closing the door,
    away from the audience,
    the onlookers,
    the prying eyes
seeking to unravel,
    to label,
seeking answers
they already know.

In the silence,
in the tender quiet,

I shed
    the expectations,
    the show,
    the forced smile,
shaking from my feet,
forced steps and too-tight shoes.

I knit myself back together,
    soaking in the music,
    a cup of hot tea in my hands,
    fuzzy white socks on my feet,
    a blanket inviting me

back into the core of myself
and the heart of my soul.

Searching

Searching for the light
of the star
we had known,
the sun passed us by
and we wondered
where had it gone,
yet we walked away
not to find the sun
had hid in its shadows
but shone in another direction.

So we walked to another star
realizing that perhaps the sun
had never meant to shine
on us at all
but we were simply on the hillside
standing in its rays
coming over the horizon,
seeing us not for the waving grass
in which we stood.

Birthed Once More

We are made of dirt
and so our bodies long to return,

casting away the barriers
lying down in the mud,
leaves against our skin

to feel once again
we are one with the earth

running with abandon
through the trees

open to all experiences,
awareness heightened

like the tall trunks

as bare feet explore
a moss-strewn floor.

Eternally Connected

Don't ever think
a day goes by
when I don't think of you.
Don't ever think
the sun treks across the sky
without me knowing
how much I've lost,
how much I had to give up
in letting you go.

Yet the bond remains
for love is not dependent
on the emotions or behavior
or even our choices.

Love simply *is*.
It is what we *are*

and so even though
life looks a little different,
the open land is new
and the constellations
are not yet my friends,

there is more space
and needed room
    to choose

and we are the same divine
beings we ever were

and love connects us all.

The Phoenix Can Rise Again

Don't give up on the dead
for the world is not what it seems

and what appears to be gone

may be simply transformed,
changed for a time
into an unrecognizable state
we do not see

unless we look with our eyes closed,
our hearts open,
to what only silence can understand.

The dead may still return
like flowers left on a grave
having taken root
and unfurling their sweet scent,
filling the air.

Standing in the Coals

Quick to laugh,
quick to cry,
forests know not our time.

They breathe,
they sing,
they burn in holy wonder

to be renewed again,
beauty in destruction
under the healing touch
of a bouquet of purple flowers
standing in the coals.

I lay my hands upon
the charcoaled wood,
on the warp and woof,
the weave of life
underlying all,

the breath of growing,

of what our hearts are saying
if only we would choose to see
beyond the dark cover
to the flowers underneath,
the eyes of our soul
which know no bounds.

New Life

Warm breezes brush my face—
a fresh new scent in the air
awakening my sight,

my desire to explore
a warm wind
filled with wild flowers:
daffodils and crocuses,

welcoming spring
like a trumpet's call
in the early morning
where I stand
proclaiming release
to the rose petaled trees

singing out,
stretching their limbs
to catch the sun's rays,

drawing out my smile,

lifting the weight
off my shoulders

into boundless possibilities.

Take the Chance

Time to embrace
the truth that you don't
have all the time
to do what you want to do
and it's not going
to be handed to you
with a signed security

so you have to let go
of your need to know
and take a risk
to *live*
and not just survive

for it's better to
take a leap off the
crystalline heights
and fall

than to have
forever lived
away from the edge,
smothered because
you could not breathe.

Take the chance.

Only Today

We constantly scramble
around in the muck of the day,
chasing after so many meaningless nothings,
forgetting the important,
constantly moving from
one small thing to the next.

We say we'll have more time tomorrow
but in truth we'll never get there
for we have made our choice
to succumb to the clatter
as days become weeks and months
and seasons turn into years.

One day you will wake up
to find life is gone
never having stopped for what truly counted
and whether by illness or accident,
or a person realizing you were never
going to give them the time,
the love you ignored is no longer here,
and the chance is taken from you
never having held her face
cherished in your hands,
what you love in your arms.

It is only then you will find
you won nothing
and lost everything
because you thought
the gift of relationship
would always be there
and you spent so much time
running after dropped coins
that you lost the diamonds.

And now I still hear you say
you will be free "tomorrow"
but I no longer believe you.
You do not have tomorrow.
You only have today
and even that is not promised.

I Love Your Face

Searching
the crowded sanctuary
under the silver cross,
I seek the look
of love
I know so well
outside
these four walls,

that tenderness
of deep affection
and strong embrace,

the smile
I close my eyes to see—
the voice
I close my ears to hear.

I wait
to catch a glimpse,
a moment of words,
an hour of silent companionship.

Your presence is here
and that alone is comforting.

I reach out my hands…

I love
your face.

Made to Love

Is it okay to love
without really knowing,
to simply throw
the desire to love
up in the air
with no expectation
for it to come down
around me
but in hopes it will join
the bigger love
I raise my voice to
crying "love!"

Love is pouring into me
and it needs somewhere to go

so is it okay that I love you—
holding your face, your voice,
your touch, and your hello
close to my chest
to remember,
to embrace and enjoy
this gift of you?

We are made to love
and so I take your hands,
so beautiful to me,
and celebrate the joy
of love without condition—
love that is flowing
from one to another
radiant, wild, and alive.

On Showing Up

As the river carries
its song to the sea
so are we carried,

for nearly
all of life
is simply a matter
of showing up—

daring to be greater,
to be a part
of something
larger than oneself
time and time again.

What Our Souls Truly Are

That's it!
Here's the magic—
the deep unknowing,
the longing of the human soul
    to laugh,
    to fly,
    to be free
high in the air,
what our souls truly are
above the illusionary chains
our minds create.

Yes! It's here!

Taking in and recognizing
what our souls know
ourselves to be,

we cry out in joyful tears
and raise our hands,

grateful for the reminder
and lost in wonder
    at the reality,
    the gift of life
    in which we find ourselves,

surrounded in love,
the light and the marvel
we always were.

The Experience Has You

You are a handful of light,
a shimmer in the wind.

As I reach out
from the tree branch
hoping to find you
there in the air,
perhaps on the heron's wing
as it rises from
the water below,

I feel my body
    pushed

and I fall from the tree,

the waves opening
to take me in,
to take me under
all conscious thought

where the light diminishes
and your divine darkness
consumes me in the depths
taken by the knowing

and when I emerge
gasping for breath
you fill me with air

taking away
all description.

Wordless Knowing

Sensing the greater reality
is an intuitive gift
but you don't always
get to say what you see.

Sometimes you have to bite your tongue
and put what is swirling
around in your heart
into your hands instead,

the deep knowing
buried ever deeper still
inside your skin
for it's not supposed to
come out of your mouth

and you have to find a way
to live it out,

this divine and unexpressed truth
like a seed hidden away
with the hope
that in its breaking,
it will find its way
through the dark earth

to one day be nourished
by the bright noonday sun
when all reality
can be known, held,
and celebrated.

Heart Open

I have found God
under a heavy rock,
in the sparkling light on the river,
and in the broken heart
of a friend.

I have heard God
in the falling rain,
the silent wind on a chilly evening,
and in the ferocious ocean's roar.

When I embrace the world—
all its beauty and all its grief,

When I look with my soul
and reach out with my hand,
touching the embodiment
of myself and another
in *all* our laughter
and *all* our tears,

I am tracing the very
face of God.

Clarity

Sometimes it seems
like I can see a picture
few others comprehend.

Where others see a grab for power,
    I see labels and destruction.

Where some see correct theology,
a God they can understand,
    I see crushed spirits
    turned away by those
    who should have seen in them
    the beautiful light of God.

Where people see opportunity,
    I see broken lives
    spent on meaningless nothing,
    a living death encapsulating their days.

Tell me, *please* tell me
how do I swim in the
overwhelming anguish I feel
from the hearts all around me
    and my own
while trying to explain to people
they are creating a hell
they believe to be heaven
and the lines of division and blame they draw
cut their own souls into shreds?

All I want to do is bring
light into the world
and it cuts me to the heart

there are those who are blind,
continually destroying themselves
and those they should treasure

and so I cry
aloud in the wilderness
through the tears of God

to those who will put ego aside for love,
hold up the gift of divine life
we've been given,

who need arms of warm embrace
and ears to hear,
for those who long to be seen with eyes
honoring their souls
and to find that truth for themselves
of all they have experienced and know

and perhaps by doing this,
perhaps by living in the compassionate
and joyous freedom God gave us,
I can help create a better light of truth,
of love, of knowing God who unites us all,
a heaven we all will experience
and want to see.

Exploring

Running my hand
along the spines
of the books
I'm longing to read

and the faces of those
with whom
I'm longing to spend the days,

each one a divine space,
God filling my senses,
speaking through
the teaching words
and the healing voices.

The pages, the skin,
the light in the eyes,
avenues of the heart
to traverse in exploration—

so many places to search,
to learn, to grow,
each one a way
to run my arms
through the depths
of the universal soul,
each one growing
me into the person
I always was
and am finding myself to be.

Along the Way

Not
all
questions

are meant
to be
answered.

Some
are for the
search.

Labyrinth of Love

This walk of love—
humbly submitting
to the way I am given

to let the silence speak
in my footsteps
and letting all I see
animate my hands,

yet my soul points
like a steady compass star
to a deeper truth
I don't fully understand

of decisions made in another time,
shaping my life
and the way I must go,

of lifting my voice
and taking others' hands
along the turns
and over the bridges
as we wind our way
on this journey
from one eternity to another

seeking the very love
flowing in our veins
and guiding us on.

Love's Truth

Like stretched out wings
connecting us all,

love's truth is the
coursing strength
integrating itself into every cell
as we sense we are more
than just ourselves,
eternal souls with greater wisdom
accompanied by the souls we lost
and the souls we know
walking with us still.

The bond—
not only in the longing
of our arms,
but in the truth
already being lived out
even as we yearn for it,

love's truth
is our reminder
nothing is ever truly divided
or travels beyond our reach.

Knowing neither labels
nor bounds,

love soars above
our limited understanding
to the reality we reach for—

the revealed soul
showing us as
sparkling lights of God

falling in love
with ourselves
again and again

just as the sun rises and sets
on each new day,
seemingly different,
yet always
coming round again

as one.

Abiding Strength

Sink into the center of abiding strength,
a calm interior at peace with itself
from which everything radiates outward

shining in every fiber with this
most mysterious and exquisite force
we call "love,"

at its core,

the living energy
ever seeking to show the
uniting of one to another
as the universe unfurls,

the hands of God
embracing through all,

sinking into the center of abiding strength,
a calm interior at peace with itself.

More Than the Word

Love—
the pearl of great price
for which you'll give
everything you can
yet it demands nothing.

It's the answer
to the hungry question
that can never be fully devoured
yet fully satisfies.

It's the light within
never burning out,
the warmth
always surrounding
and the joy
flowing everlasting.

Love is the only gift
you can never buy
yet when it's given…
when it's held out
and openly embraced,
it's the one thing
you'll never want to let go.

Love is the life
in which we *live*.

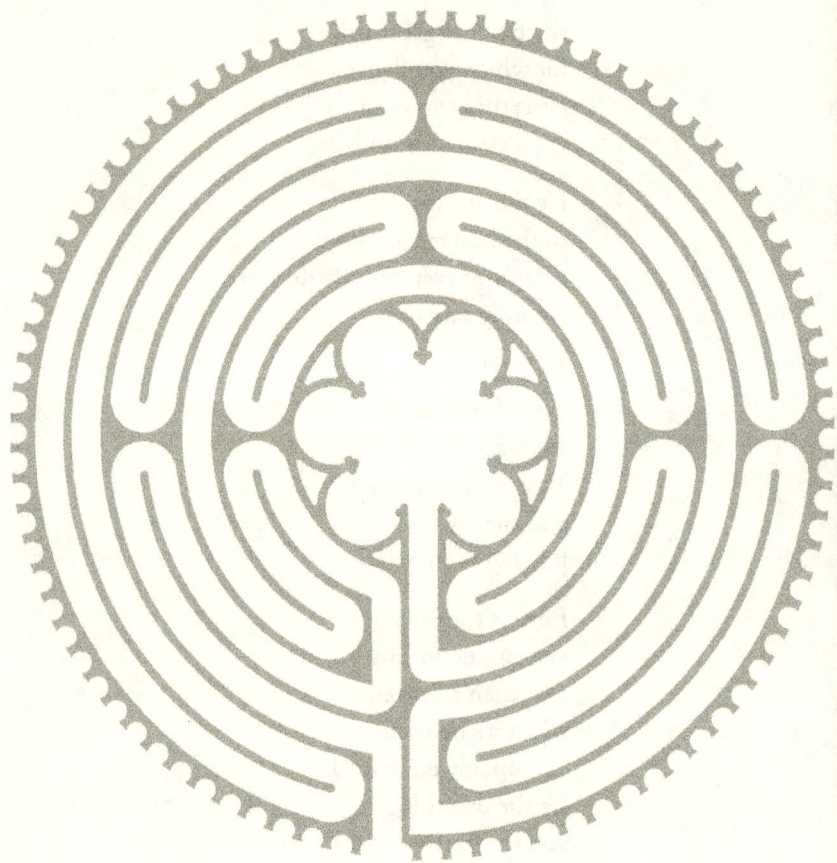